The Baker's Craft

A Short History

A.M. Steve Volk

THE BAKER'S CRAFT
A SHORT HISTORY

iUniverse books may be ordered through booksellers or by contacting:

iUniverse
1663 Liberty Drive
Bloomington, IN 47403
www.iuniverse.com
1-800-Authors (1-800-288-4677)

Because of the dynamic nature of the Internet, any web addresses or links contained in this book may have changed since publication and may no longer be valid. The views expressed in this work are solely those of the author and do not necessarily reflect the views of the publisher, and the publisher hereby disclaims any responsibility for them.

Any people depicted in stock imagery provided by Getty Images are models, and such images are being used for illustrative purposes only. Certain stock imagery © Getty Images.

ISBN: 978-1-5320-6025-0 (sc)
ISBN: 978-1-5320-6026-7 (e)

Library of Congress Control Number: 2018912129

Print information available on the last page.

iUniverse rev. date: 10/10/2018

THE BAKERS CRAFT - A SHORT HISTORY

by

Adolph M. (Steve) Volk

Of all foods, none is so closely linked with the course of human history as bread. Breadmaking commenced when primitive man first pounded edible grains between two large stones, mixing the resultant meal with water and baking the mixture on hot, flat stones. It is interesting at this point to note the direct linkage between the primitive hot stone and the modern hot plate.

It has always been accepted that the first reference to a baker in history is contained in the 40th chapter of Genesis. It refers to Pharaoh's chief baker, who was hanged. The words "chief baker" seems proof of the fact that baking had been established as a craft and was not solely a domestic practice.

It was the chance discovery of a cuneiform tablet some years ago that changed this conception, for, when it was deciphered, an earlier baker stepped out into history. The language was Sumarian and the date was established at approximately 2366 B.C. It recorded the delivery of grain for Numbari and others, the list including 180 measures of grain for Luga the baker; so Luga who practiced the arts of milling and baking in ancient Babylonia over 4,300 years ago was delivered not only of corn but, by virtue of the recording tablet from oblivion. The tablet is now in the Ashmolian Museum in Oxford.

It is know that bread was made in the Paleolithic period, for stone ovens of that age have been discovered in Smyrna, Evidence of breadmaking in the Neolithic age is provided by the discovery of ovens in Egypt which were of the first and second dynasties, 3188 - 2815 B.C.

New technology doesn't always squelch old traditions, sometimes it leads us back to them. When bread machines arrived on the scene a decade ago they made homemade loaves an everyday possibility instead of a rare pleasure. Now machines are better and cheaper. The new models make larger, conventionally shaped loaves. A hand shaped loaf is an option, thanks to dough cycles. The machine does the sticky work, you shape the loaf and pop it in the oven.

Today consumers are looking for healthy, nutritious breads. Today's market has more than 35 complete bread mixes available. There also are cholesterol and fat free breads. Some favor breads such as the San Francisco hard crust or multigrain breads made up of a blend of flour and seeds. These healthy loaves are natural partners for salads and soft cheese. You can vary your seed proportions, using different varieties of seeds. It is important, however, to keep the seed amount no higher than 60%, based on flour weight or else the texture of the bread will become too sandy and course.

IT'S A GINGERBREAD HOLIDAY!!!

To, Mr. Steve Volk,

The best thing about Gingerbread is the sharing. People create gingerbread houses to make other people smile.

The first Gingerbread Man is believed to have been made at the court of Queen Elizabeth I, who favored important visitors with gingerbread likenesses of themselves.

A cookbook published in 1615 gives the full details of how a *"course Gingerbread"* was made in those days:

Take a quart of honie and set it on the coales and refine it; then take a pennyworth of ginger, as much pepper, as much Licoris, and a quarter of a pound of Aniseedes, and a pennyworth of Saunders (red sandalwood): All these must be beaten and seared, and so put up the hony; then put in a quarter of a pint of claret wine and strow it amongst the rest; and stirre it till it come to a stiffe paste, and then make it into cakes and drie them gently.

(Gervase Markham, "The English Hus-wife")

Gradually, molasses and flour replaced the honey and bread crumbs, making a dark, rich gingerbread.

When the Grimm Brothers collected German fairy tales, they found out about Hansel and Gretel, two children who, abandoned in the woods by destitute parents, discovered a house made of bread, cake and candies.

Christmas has always been the most popular season for gingerbread. German bakeries began offering fancy gingerbread houses with icing snow on the roofs during the 19th century.

Original Wedding Cake Prices, By Volks, Many Years Ago, In Los Gatos, Saratoga, & Sacramento, California.

I Started Doing Wedding Cakes, While Serving In The
#1 Air Force (1950) At Elemadorf A.F.B. Anchorage AK
#2 Mitchel A.F.B. Officer Club, Gold Room & NCO Club
#3 First Wedding Cake, At The Air Force Academy CO.

CATEGORY		I	II	III	IV
Servings	**Size of Cake Rounds**	**2.25**	**2.55**	**2.95**	**3.95**
53	6", 10"	119.25	135.15	156.35	209.35
80	8", 12"	180.00	206.55	238.95	319.95
102	6", 9", 12"	229.50	260.10	300.90	402.90
130	6", 10", 14"	292.50	331.50	383.50	513.50
180	8", 12", 16"	405.00	461.55	533.95	714.95
202	6", 9", 12", 16"	454.50	515.10	595.90	797.90
257	6", 10", 14", 18" with base	578.25	655.35	758.15	1015.15
364	6", 9", 12", 16", 20"	819.00	928.20	1073.80	1437.80
497	6", 10", 14", 18", 24"	1118.25	1267.35	1466.15	1963.15
583	8", 12", 16", 20", 24"	1311.75	1486.65	1719.85	2302.85
604	6", 9", 12", 16", 20", 24"	1359.00	1540.20	1781.80	2385.80
Servings	**Single Round Cakes**	**2.25**	**2.55**	**2.95**	**3.95**
14	6"	31.50	35.70	41.30	55.30
24	8"	54.00	61.20	70.80	94.80
32	9"	72.00	81.60	94.40	126.40
39	10"	87.75	99.45	115.05	154.05
56	12"	126.00	142.80	165.20	221.20
77	14"	173.25	196.35	227.15	304.15
100	16"	225.00	255.00	295.00	395.00
127	18" Base	285.75	323.85	374.65	501.65
162	20" Base	364.50	413.10	477.90	639.90
240	24" Base	540.00	612.00	708.00	948.00

Resources for Baking Educators

www.rbanet.com   RBA's home page is changing and growing. Bookmark us for future stops. Look for new files on certification, Commercial Baking Contest VICA, baking curriculum and links to organizations and schools.

www.aibonline.org   American Institute of Baking offers a variety of resident course, self-study, research and even certification in the areas of bakery management, sciences, sanitation and safety.

www.bbga.org   The Bread Baker's Guild of America is the site for information about traditional breads. Their page has a neat section on bread books you may want to review. BBG will conduct a half dozen seminars at RBA's annual convention - Marketplace 99.

www.vica.org   There are about 14,000 Vocational Industrial Clubs of American Chapters. RBA is the sponsor of the National Commercial Baking Contest held at Skills USA-VICA each June. Log on to learn more about the Skills USA, as well as the Baking and Culinary competitions

www.fhahero.com   There are about 8,500 Future Homemakers of America chapters. FHA hosts national foodservice competition - check out Programs/ STAR events.

www.nacufs.org   The National Association of College and University Food Services. Lots of interesting links to publications, job bulletin, and networks.

www.dunwoody.tec.mn.us/nbc/nbc.htm The National Baking Center is devoted exclusively to traditional scratch baking. Educators wanting an eye opening experience about the effects of flour, mixing method and bench work on bread quality or who just want to work in a state of the art bakery need to sign on today.

www.pastrychef.com   Interesting web site. The best features are the "Ask the Pastry Chef" and the "Directory of Baking Sites".

www.vpw.com   Video Placement Worldwide distributes free, permanent loan videos to secondary and postsecondary programs. Log on the Partnership page to read about RBA's baking career video, Switching Channels. Order your copy today – it's free.

http://stats.bls.gov is the Bureau of Labor Statistics home page, and http://stats.bls.gov/oes/oes_data.htm is their file for occupational stats. You may find this site useful when writing your next grant, or preparing your Orientation lecture.

Foodservice Educators Network International (FENI)

Its mission is to partner with foodservice educators (high school, training centers, job corp, corporate trainers, and colleges) to advance professional growth and culinary/baking education. Services include a newsletter and educational summit (January). There are plans for identifying best practices based on the Baldrige Award standards for education, professional development scholarships, and other informational resources. For more information about FENI please contact Mary Petersen: telephone 410-268-5542, fax 410-263-3110 or e-mail to EAHX15A@Prodigy.com.

If you are planning on a first class location such as a strip mall, beware of the additional expenses in addition to rent. I did better in the basement of a very old store. More details about that in the following pages.

1	Capitol Neon Sign Cake & Cooky Co.	$2,280.00
2	Custom Made Front Window Base Cabinet for Window Case	4,880.00
3	Custom Made Frame W/Glass Doors for Window Case	1,500.00
4	Custom Lighted Canopy (Per Plan) With Five Spotlights and Timer	2,480.00
5	Calwest (New) Fire Protection Engineering. Entire Store Sprinklers.	875.00
6	Upper Wall Trim Around Front of Store 48 ft. Canopy	1,680.00
7	Six Section Back Wall Shelving W/Mirror and Cabinet	5,016.00
8	Floodlights Installed Custom Made Baro Lighting Upgrade	472.00
9	Large Full-size Wall to Ceiling Mirror (Front) On Side Wall	535.00
10	Custom Made Cookie Case - Mercury Equip. Co. Of Los Angeles	4,600.00
11	Custom Made Bakery Case (Dry) For Cookies & Pastries	7,800.00
12	Custom Made Self-Service Corner Counter	275.00
13	Custom Made Refrigerated Bakery Case. Cakes & Pastries.	8,500.00
14	Custom Made Euro Candy Case (Disconnected) As Is Condition	5,800.00
15	Custom Made Box Wrap Station W/Cabinet	3,300.00
16	Custom Canopy With 19 Installed Lights	1,680.00
17	Custom Swing Gate Between Counter W/Book Stand	200.00
18	Nubs Cash Register (On Counter) On Back Wall	635.16
19	Master Card With I.D. Credit Check Machine Set-up $125.00	1,952.50
20	Hammon Floor Fashion, Tile By The Door, Behind Counter & Bakery	3,090.00
21	Hammon Floor Fashion Rug In Front of Bakery Counter	1,052.00
22	(3) S.E. Rykoff Red Mats and (10) Stress Rubber Mats	366.91
23	(3) S.E. Rykoff Customer's Green Plastic Tables 24" by 24"	155.10
24	(6) S.E. Rykoff Customer's Green Plastic Chairs	117.00
25	Traulsen Three Door Refrigerator Case (S.N. #T06970)	3,475.00
26	Traulsen Three Door Freezer Case (S.N. #T161390)	4,257.00
27	Traulsen Six Sections # Four Pan Sliders For Refrig. & Freezer	1,116.00
28	(2) Aluminum Sheet Pan Rack on Wheels	358.00
29	(75) Westco Alum. Sheet Pans Sixteen Gauge (18" x 26") 11.50 ea.	862.50
30	Bakery Table (Hard Wood) With Side Boards 3' by 5' W/shelf	465.00
31	Two Double Stack Convection Ovens, Four Working Ovens	11,980.00
32	Two Compartment Bakery Pan Sink (State Regulation)	890.00

Culinary Externship Program

Student's Name _____   Date _____ Thru _____

Social Security #: _____   Home Phone _____

School _____   School Phone _____

Basic Student's Evaluation	Review 0 - 2	Average 3 - 5	Above 6 - 8	Excellent 9 - 10	Completed Hours	Dates
Safety & Sanitation						
Cooperation						
Initiatives						
Tools & Equipment						
Machines & Ovens						
Weights & Measures						
Counter & Telephone						
Delivery & Set Ups						
Culinary Projects						
Mixing & Bench						
Bread & Rolls						
Danish & Pastries						
Cookies & Fruit Bars						
Cakes & Icings						
Ganache & Fondant						
Cake Dec. Borders						
Roses, Buds & Leaves						
Kopy Kake/Spray Guns						
Party Cakes/Decorating						
Wedding Cakes/Set Ups						

Total Score: Out of 200 Points (_____)   Dates Absent _____, _____, _____, _____

Instructor Signatures: _____   _____

           Adolph (Steve) Volk, A.C.F.

Student Signature: _____   Date Completed _____

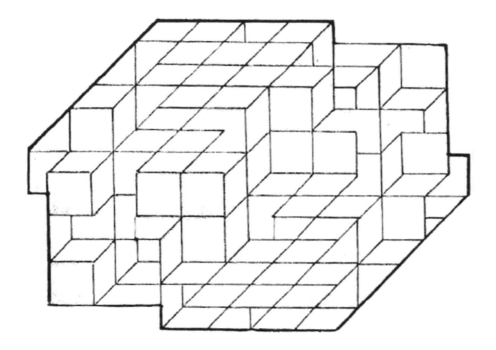

This is only one of many projects I have, In training students, with problems seeing their colors Using all dark colors, Red & green are the same color. Copyright (C) A.M. STEVE VOLK 1967

Exchange the squares above to 8x11". Place on a cardboard with tracing paper taped on top. Use black piping gel and outline the boxes for steady and straight lines. Students will mix and use six different colors in an 8 oz. cup and fill in the squares with no matching colors to be side by side. To start place a color dot into each square, using yellow, red, green and blue for the base colors. With 4 oz. of piping gel in a 8 oz. cup add colors by the teaspoon. To change colors add one of each: yellow & red = orange/ yellow & blue = green/red & blue = purple/red & green = brown. Light or dark, place two tablespoons in a paper cone and cut a small tip. Set a time limit whether finished or not. Place all the 8x11" papers on the table to compare. Students should comment on their work and their colors. This is a good test and gives ideas about colors to work with and how to mix.

I have retired from baking, after owning three bakeries in Los Gatos, Saratoga & Sacramento. Also teaching at three collages, West Valley 16 years, Canada 8 years & Pacific Coast 2 years. Last (SETA) Bakers Hand Craft Training for 6 years, For unemployed, welfare, with no skills. Mentor, for San Jose High School For 8 years. Mentor, Federal & State Prisons & Juvey Hall. Also for 9 years of my military 20 years service I was /Sgt, N.C.O.I.C. Baker Instructor, also Executive Pastry Chef, for many V.V.I.P.

While in the service, I was entered into many culinary shows with the military culinary teams. After retirement, I enjoyed entering culinary shows with my students, wining their culinary ribbons & trophy's. It was worth their training. I can say teaching students all the culinary item they would need, To move ahead and work with the culinary art they could do best. From Baker To Cake Decorating and Wedding Cakes, Icing Flowers, Tail Bread Art, Gingerbread Houses & Basic, Pulled Sugar Art, & Ice Sculptures, Etc.

World Association of Chefs Societies

The World Association of Chefs Societies, or Worldchefs, is a global network of chefs associations founded in October 1928 at the Sorbonne in Paris. At that first congress there were 65 delegates from 17 countries, representing 36 national and international associations. August Escoffier was named the first honorary president of Worldchefs.

Today, this global body has 93 official chefs associations as members that represent over 10 million professional chefs worldwide. The biennial congress is a hallmark tradition of Worldchefs and has been organized in more than 20 cities across the world throughout its 82-year history.

Worldchefs is a non-political professional organization dedicated to maintaining and improving the culinary standards of global cuisines through education, training and professional development of its international membership. As an authority and opinion leader on food, Worldchefs represents a global voice on all issues related to the culinary profession.

ADOLPH (STEVE) VOLK, AAC
California Capitol Chefs Association
Chapter of the American Culinary Federation

PROFESSIONAL
MEMBERSHIP

American Academy of Chefs (Honor Society)
Certified Executive Pastry Chef, ACF-CEPC (Life)
Certified Culinary Educator ACF (Life)-CCE
Retail Bakers of America-Master Baker (Life) CMB
International Cake Exploration Societe & CA Chapter
1976 Culinary Olympics Gold Medal Winner, Germany

EDUCATION

West Valley College, Saratoga CA   Major Chefs Training
San Jose College, San Jose CA   Major Art Classes
Canada College, Redwood City CA   Major Food Service
University of California, Berkeley   Major Voc Ed Instructor
Sacramento State, Sacramento CA   Major Education & Art

CREDENTIALS

Culinary Arts Instructor (CA State License) Life
Bureau of Industrial Education, 1967 (Life) No. 3589 VTP
Standard Teaching Credential (Life) 1967, File 3786-90 kt
California Private Postsecondary Credential, No. 44159

SPECIAL
CLASSES

Culinary Institute of America 1960, Air Force Culinary Scholarship

Statler Hilton, Waldorf Astoria & Governor Clinton Hotels - 1200 hours
Advance Hotel Training 1953-1955, New York & Chicago - 480 hours
1955 Research Formulas (major companies) Chicago - 320 hours
Quartermasters Chef 1948, Quartermasters Baker 1949, Military School

AWARDS
(While teaching)
1968-1988

Culinary Olympic Gold Medal, Germany 1976
Special Recognition, Culinary Olympics, Germany 1984 & 1988
Worlds Fair, Vancouver BC, Silver & Bronze Medals
McCormick Place Chicago (CA team) USA, 3rd place 1975

AWARDS
(While in AF)
1950-1962

Geneva Culinaire & Pan American Awards 1962
Societe Culinaire Philanthropique, New York - France
Won national & international awards 1952-1961
Air Force (individual) culinary trophy 1960
World Food Conference 1959, PA. Total 10 awards
United Nations Award, silver, 1958, NY. Total 6 awards

SPECIAL ASSIGNMENTS	Exec. Pastry Chef, Ice Carvings, Catering, Cake Decorator
	Pres. Harry S. Truman, 1948, Kirtland AFB, Albequerque NM
	Pres. Dwight D. Eisenhower, 1955. Opening of AF Academy, Denver CO
	Pres. John F. Kennedy, 1962, Egland AFB, Ft. Walton Beach FL
MILITARY SERVICE	VP Lyndon Johnson, 1962, Egland AFB & Washington Death Care
	Headquarters Alaska Air Command (Chateau) Anchorage AK
US Navy 1942-1946 US Air Force 1946-1962 Disabled Veteran	Bob Hope w/TV & Hollywood All Star Troops, USO events
	His Eminence Cardinal Spellman, Kruchev of Russia I, Mary Martin, Marilyn Monroe, Jane Mansfield, Dean Martin, Sammy Davis, Jr., Jerry Lewis, etc. Headquarters Continental Air Command, Mitchel Field NY & United Nations
Retired 100% disability	NY. Princess Grace of Monaco as well as other known personalities. *As pastry chef I had the privilege of meeting and serving the names above.*

The Retail Bakers of America and its
Officers and Directors hereby certify that

Adolph (STEVE) Volk

has successfully fulfilled the requirements for
designation as a Master Baker under the
RBA Master Baker Certification Program.

June 1987

Hans B. Madlin
President

Richard C. Bohlas
Executive Vice President

Richard M. Pflueger Jr.
Chairman, Apprenticeship &
Training Committee

14

CERTIFICATE OF AUTHORIZATION
FOR SERVICE

in a California Private Postsecondary Educational Institution
Issued by the Council for Private Postsecondary and Vocational Education
Pursuant to California Education Code Section 94311(a)(3)
Authorization Document Number: 11887

LAST NAME:	VOLK	FIRST NAME:	ADOLPH	MIDDLE INITIAL: M.	DATE: 8/91
ADDRESS:	5489 C - SUNRISE BLVD.				TELEPHONE 916:965-5448
CITY:	CITRUS HEIGHTS	STATE: CA	ZIP CODE: 95610		

Please check appropriate box: ADMINISTRATOR   INSTRUCTOR

List the subjects you will teach: _____ CULINARY ARTS _____

THIS CERTIFICATE OF AUTHORIZATION FOR SERVICE IS VALID ONLY AT A CALIFORNIA PRIVATE POSTSECONDARY EDUCATIONAL INSTITUTION WHICH HAS OCCUPATIONAL COURSES APPROVED BY THE COUNCIL FOR PRIVATE POSTSECONDARY AND VOCATIONAL EDUCATION PURSUANT TO CALIFORNIA EDUCATION CODE SECTION 94311(a)(3). THIS AUTHORIZATION IDENTIFIES THE INDIVIDUAL HOLDER AND VERIFIES THAT THE HOLDER POSSESS ADEQUATE ACADEMIC, EXPERIENTIAL, AND PROFESSIONAL QUALIFICATIONS AS DEFINED BY THE EDUCATION CODE. THIS DOCUMENT DOES NOT AUTHORIZE AN INDIVIDUAL TO OPERATE AS, OR INDEPENDENTLY OF, AN EDUCATIONAL INSTITUTION.

Kenneth A. Miller, Executive Director
Council for Private Postsecondary
and Vocational Education

ADDRESS INQUIRIES TO: Authorizations Desk
Council for Private Postsecondary
and Vocational Education
1027 10th Street, 4th Floor
Sacramento, CA 95814
Telephone: (916) 327-6900

COUNCIL FOR PRIVATE POSTSECONDARY
AND VOCATIONAL EDUCATION
1027 10th Street, Fourth Floor
Sacramento, CA 95814

You might apply for this license if you intend to teach externship from another culinary school in your bake shop. Also for those who don't have a teaching license, but want to teach adult education in the local Jr. College or Recreation Dept.

A.M. Steve Volk shows how one can 'Learn to Earn'
New book directs readers to life of success, joy with real-life insights, inspiration

FAIR OAKS, Calif. - Award-winning chef and instructor A.M. Steve Volk returns to the publishing scene with a new book teaching readers how one can "Learn to Earn" (published by AuthorHouse). Insightful and inspirational, this guide combines tips to ace in culinary art and food service with valuable career advancement advice, all taken from his personal success story.

It has always been Volk's goal to teach the basics in culinary art and food service. "Learn to Earn" is the perfect vehicle to realize his goals. Through its pages, aspiring chefs and others who dream of making it big in this industry will find tips, suggestions and inspiration to pursue their dreams.

"'Learn to Earn is not a hand down, or a hand out, but a hand up from low wages or unemployment to learning a trade of your liking, becoming skillful at your trade, and earning a living," Volk points out.

With today's rise in the unemployment rate, the author, through "Learn to Earn," calls for every individual to take part in a transformative experience of redirecting a challenging and stressful life to one of joy and success. He emphasizes: "You are never too old to learn!"

Sampling is the best part of baking.

I need a smaller rolling pin, or more dough.

CERTIFICATE OF AUTHORIZATION
FOR SERVICE

in a California Private Postsecondary Educational Institution
Issued by the Council for Private Postsecondary and Vocational Education
Pursuant to California Education Code Section 94311(a)(3)
Authorization Document Number: 11887

LAST NAME:	VOLK	FIRST NAME:	ADOLPH	MIDDLE INITIAL: M.	DATE: 8/91
ADDRESS	5489 C - SUNRISE BLVD.				TELEPHONE 916·965-5448
CITY:	CITRUS HEIGHTS	STATE CA	ZIP CODE 95610		

Please check appropriate box: ADMINISTRATOR   INSTRUCTOR

List the subjects you will teach: _____ CULINARY ARTS _____

THIS CERTIFICATE OF AUTHORIZATION FOR SERVICE IS VALID ONLY AT A CALIFORNIA PRIVATE POSTSECONDARY EDUCATIONAL INSTITUTION WHICH HAS OCCUPATIONAL COURSES APPROVED BY THE COUNCIL FOR PRIVATE POSTSECONDARY AND VOCATIONAL EDUCATION PURSUANT TO CALIFORNIA EDUCATION CODE SECTION 94311(a)(3). THIS AUTHORIZATION IDENTIFIES THE INDIVIDUAL HOLDER AND VERIFIES THAT THE HOLDER POSSESS ADEQUATE ACADEMIC, EXPERIENTIAL, AND PROFESSIONAL QUALIFICATIONS AS DEFINED BY THE EDUCATION CODE. THIS DOCUMENT DOES NOT AUTHORIZE AN INDIVIDUAL TO OPERATE AS, OR INDEPENDENTLY OF, AN EDUCATIONAL INSTITUTION.

Kenneth A. Miller, Executive Director
Council for Private Postsecondary
and Vocational Education

ADDRESS INQUIRIES TO: Authorizations Desk
Council for Private Postsecondary
and Vocational Education
1027 10th Street, 4th Floor
Sacramento, CA 95814
Telephone: (916) 327-8900

COUNCIL FOR PRIVATE POSTSECONDARY
AND VOCATIONAL EDUCATION
1027 10th Street, Fourth Floor
Sacramento, CA 95814

You might apply for this license if you intend to teach externship
from another culinary school in your bake shop. Also for those who
don't have a teaching license, but want to teach adult education in the
local Jr. College or Recreation Dept.

We are hoping to learn by doing.

It could use a little more flour,

I need some flour for the rolling pin.

Can we each bake. Two nights a month.

Also cook dinner, For you & dad, To learn.

Are next lesson is in your cake decorating

classes, You can practicing on us to start.?

T/Sgt A.M. Steve Volk
100% Disable Veteran
5115 Rimwood Dr
Fair Oaks, CA 95628

Now I Am In Need Of Some Information, (From Anyone,) That Is Teaching Children, From The Ages (6 To 17) Also Training Young Intern Chefs, In Classes Ages 18 To 23-25, In Culinary Art, /Cooking, /Baking, /Cake Decorating. Etc. In High School 9th Thru 12th / Collage 13th Thru 16th / Also Adult Culinary Education, / Privet Schools & Academy Etc

The Name Of My Next Book #7 (Children In Kitchen)
 (1). Photos Of The Classroom & Their Culinary Art Work.
 (2). Parents Permission To Have Their Photo In The Book, > Under The Age Of 18, All Above 18 There Permission.
 (3). Culinary Achievements, Use Only There First Names.
 (4). The Name Of Your School, And Your Addresses, Map
 (5). Subject, Time, Cost, Material Needed, & Work Tools.
 (6). Other Classes. When, & Name Of The Instructor.
 (7). Advance Privet Classes, Too Become A Better Chef,

 ➤ Ice Sculptures, Pull & Blown Sugar, Chocolate Work
 ➤ Salt Sculptures, Bread Weaving, (The List Is Endless)

American Culinary Federation

Educational Institute

Adolph M. Volk

Certified Executive Pastry Chef

American Culinary Federation

Educational Institute

Adolph M. Volk

Certified Culinary Educator

Life

This is to Certify

Adolph (Steve) Volk

ADOLPH M. VOLK

has been awarded

One of our Members, Steve Volk, C.P.C.
won the SILVER and BRONZE awards at the Worlds'
Fair held in Vancouver for his pastry presentations

Baked Foods Competition

Pacific Bakers Exhibition

B. C. Place

Awarded this 11th day of August 1986

Official Judge

Committee Chairman

Committee Chairman

· ·
PACIFIC BAKERS EXHIBITION 1986
B.C. PLACE (the heart of EXPO 86)
Vancouver, British Columbia, Canada
August 11, 12, and 13, 1986

Adolph (Steve) Volk AAC World Culinary Olympics Award

Internationale Kochkunst-Ausstellung, Frankfurt, Germany
Awarded 1976 Culinary Olympic Gold Medal
Awarded 1984 Culinary Olympic Diploma of Honor
Awarded 1988 Culinary Olympic Culinary Excellence

picture 026 - Paint

Adolph (Steve) Volk AAC World Culinary Olympics Award

Internationale Kochkunst-Ausstellung, Frankfurt, Germany
Awarded 1976 Culinary Olympic Gold Medal
Awarded 1984 Culinary Olympic Diploma of Honor
Awarded 1988 Culinary Olympic Culinary Excellence

Being the youngest & the only boy, With four older sisters,
Who will be Learning first to cook like my mom.

Being the youngest & the only boy,
With four older sisters, Who will be
Learning first to cook like my mom.

As you can see in all the photos, I am the youngest of my sisters, Doing all the mixing, Mom help.

…gest & the onlyoy,
our older sisters, Who wl be
Learning first to cook like my mom.

FIRST PRIZE at the National Hotel Exposition in New York was recently won by S/Sgt. Adolph M. Volk of Elmendorf AFB. Alaska,

CLASS D GROUP 1
SUGAR WORK

SCALE MODEL OF STERNWHEELER
AT FAIRBANKS, ALASKA
PREPARED AT ELMENDORF APB
AND TRAVELED 4,099 MILES

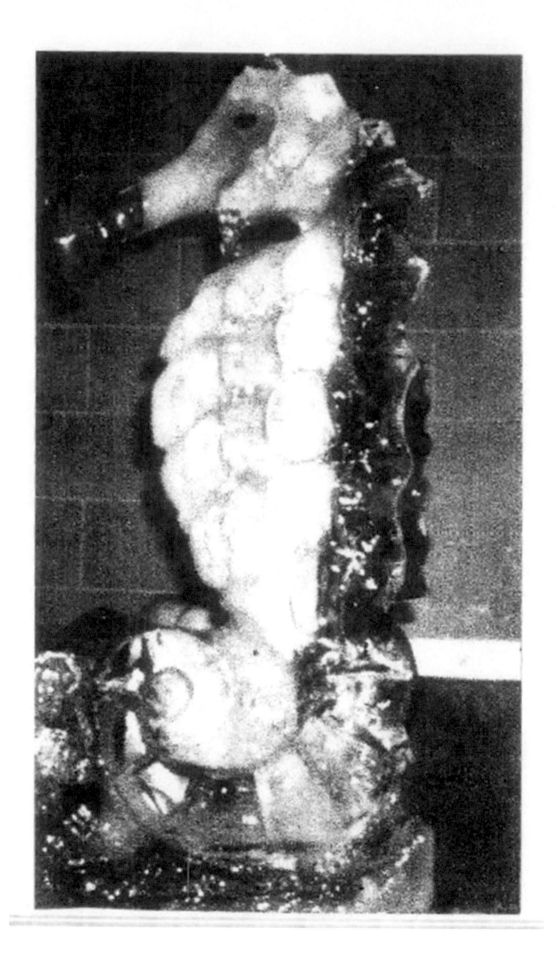

This "walk-thru" wedding cake was most challenging. The bride wanted to be able to walk under her cake. If you are interested in doing one, two stainless pipes run through two 55 gallon barrels. Holding up the top of the cake is a ¾ inch plywood board. The guests were flown in from various parts of the country. The Italian dinner was the best I have ever eaten. Quite the wedding.

This "walk-thru" wedding cake was most challenging. The bride wanted to be able to walk under her cake. If you are interested in doing one, two stainless pipes run through two 55 gallon barrels. Holding up the top of the cake is a ¾ inch plywood board. The guests were flown in from various parts of the country. The Italian dinner was the best I have ever eaten. Quite the wedding.

TEXT, EXAMS, AND PROJECT CLASSES
Total Time • 360 Hours

<u>Module I: 4 Weeks (120 Hrs.)</u>   <u>Module II: 4 Weeks (120 Hrs.)</u>   <u>Module III: 4 Weeks (120 Hrs.)</u>

Module I

	Hours
<u>Lecture* (For New Students)</u>	
Entrance Exam	2
Expectations & Goals	3
School Policies	2
School Staff & Students	2
Curriculum Procedures	<u>3</u>
TOTAL	**12**

Text Practical Baking	Hours
Sanitation & Safety	3½
Appendix Review	2½
Ingredients & Properties	6
TOTAL	12

	Hours
Review and Exams	12
Slide Projector	12

<u>Hands On/Include Demo</u>	Hours
Making Paper Cones	4
Coloring Transparent Gel	2
Setting Up Gel Projects	4
5 Square Project with Gel	4½
Straight and Curved Lines	4½
Writing and Overpiping	3½
Stems, Leaves and Bows	<u>1½</u>
TOTAL	**24**
Kopy Kake Machine	2½
Silkscreen Cake Art	5

Module II

<u>Lecture</u>	Hours
New Students Review*	12
Orientation Objectives	1½
Class Responsibilities	1½
Importance of Recipes	1½
Research of Information	<u>1½</u>
TOTAL	**18**

Chapter II thru VI	Hours
Bread & Rolls	8
Sweet Dough	5
Biscuits & Muffins	1½
Donuts & Pies	<u>9½</u>
TOTAL	24

	Hours
Review and Exams	12
Slide Projector	12

<u>Hands On/Include Demo</u>	Hours
Demo Sugar Molding	2½
Practice • White Sugar Only	4½
Pre-Color Sugar Molding	1
Cast Sugar From Molds	6
3 Easter Egg Shells	<u>4</u>
TOTAL	**18**
Royal Icing Demo	3
Deco Whip Royal	1½
Egg White with Lemon	<u>1½</u>
TOTAL	**6**

Module III

<u>Lecture</u>	Hours
New Students Review*	12
Review of Skills Learned	1½
Setting up Resumes	4½
TOTAL	**18**

Chapter VII thru IX	Hours
Cake Specialties	7
Cookies	4
Special Baking	8
Copying Recipes	<u>5</u>
	24

	Hours
Review and Exams	12
Slide Projector	12

<u>Hands On/Include Demo</u>	Hours
Demo Care of Molds	1
Demo Dark Chocolate	2½
Color White Chocolate	<u>2½</u>
TOTAL	**6**
Chocolate Easter Eggs	6
Chocolate Molding	6
White and Color Molding	6
Leaves, Cut-outs, Cones	6
Boxes, Boats, Tart Shells	<u>6</u>
TOTAL	**30**

Air Gun Atomizer	4½					
	TOTAL	12	Royal Lace & Canilli	6	Demo Mixing Marzipan	1½
			Royal String Work	6	Work Plain Marzipan	4½
Piping Gel Transfers on Tracing Paper		12	TOTAL	12	Mold and Shape w/ Color	12
					TOTAL	18
			Decorate Easter Eggs	18		
		120		120		120

Check out the list of "What Ifs". One can go without food for several weeks, but not without water for 3 to 7 days. Family preparation for survival is important. Of course there will always to those who are never prepared and will be in need. Extras supplies are never lost. Be prepared!

BAKESHOP - BAKERY CLASSROOM
Total Time • 360 Hours

Module IV: 4 Weeks (120 Hours)		Module V: 4 Weeks (120 Hours)		Module VI: 4 Weeks (120 Hours)	
	Hours		Hours		Hours
Lecture		**Lecture**		**Lecture**	
Safety & Sanitation	2	Safety & Sanitation	2	Safety & Sanitation	2
Weights & Measures	5	Weights & Measures	5	Weights & Measures	5
Orientation (For week)	4	Orientation (For week)	4	Orientation (For week)	4
Objectives (For day)	4	Objectives (For day)	4	Objectives (For day)	4
Ingredients, Types	25	Food Cost & Controls	25	Bake Shop Equipment	25
TOTAL	40	TOTAL	40	TOTAL	40
Demo with Lecture		**Demo with Lecture**		**Demo with Lecture**	
Safety of Donut Fryer	1	Safety, Use of Sheeder	1	Safety, Use of Gas Equip.	1
Baking Procedures	4	Baking Procedures	4	Baking Procedures	4
Weights & Measures	4	Weights & Measures	4	Weights & Measures	4
Yeast Breads Make-up White Pan Bread	15	Yeast Breads Make-up Dark, Grain, Etc.	15	Yeast Breads Make-up Sout, French, Etc.	15
TOTAL	24	TOTAL	24	TOTAL	24
Hands On Production		**Hands On Production**		**Hands On Production**	
Danish (Yeast)	8	Sweet Rolls (Yeast)	6	Puff Pastries (Roll In)	8
Dinner Rolls (Yeast)	4	Quick Breads & Muffins	4	Coffee Cake Rolls/Sheets	5
White & Marble Cake	4	Chocolate & Spice Cake	4	Sponge & Carrot Cake	8
Cup Cakes & Toppings	3	Fruit Bars & Nut Bars	6	Icebox & Fancy Cookies	4
Bock Icing	4	Butter Cream Icing	4	Fondant Icing	4
Bake Shop Cookies	4	Florentinas	4	Jelly Rolls	4
Beehive Cake	2	Florentinos Cake	5	Napoleans	4
Press Cake	4	Matterhorns	3	Rainbow Rem & Snowballs	3
Petit Fours	3	Swedish Blondes	3	Chocolate Krispies & Moon Rocks	3
Swedish Tart Mazarn	3	Cherry Rounds	3	Fruit Squares	3
In-store Cookies	3	Fancy Butter Cookies	2	Truffle Round	3
Pie Fillings & Dough	6	Fillings & Turnovers	4	Fruit & Sheetpan Squares	4
Yeast Donuts	8	Cake Donuts	8	Fancy Donuts	3
TOTAL	56	TOTAL	56	TOTAL	56
GRAND TOTAL	120	**GRAND TOTAL**	120	**GRAND TOTAL**	120

Special Classroom and Homework Projects: Six Holiday Drawings, Tail and Salt Bread Art, Fondant and Doll Cake, Panoramic Easter Egg, Gingerbread House, (One Step) Speed Roses, Specd (In-Store) Cakes, Speed Wedding Cakes

CULINARY ARTS AND FINE PASTRIES
Total Time • 360 Hours

	Hours		Hours		Hours
Lectures		**Lectures**		**Lectures**	
Safety & Sanitation	2	Safety & Sanitation	2	Safety & Sanitation	2
Orientation (For week)	4	Orientation (For week)	4	Orientation (For week)	4
Objective (For day)	4	Objective (For day)	4	Objective (For day)	4
Recipes for Projects	6	Recipes for Projects	6	Recipes for Projects	6
On-going Guidelines	6	On-going Guidelines	6	On-going Guidelines	6
TOTAL	22	TOTAL	22	TOTAL	22
Introduction To:		**Introduction To:**		**Introduction To:**	
Spun Sugar Art	6	??? Sugar Art	6	Pulled Sugar Wrap	6
Hot Pulled Sugar	6	Burnt Black Gold	6	Pulled Sugar Ribbon	6
Clear Block Sugar	6	Colored Black Sugar	6	Pulled Sugar Flowers	6
TOTAL	18	TOTAL	18	TOTAL	18
Demo with Lectures		**Demo with Lectures**		**Demo with Lectures**	
Butter Cream Borders	2	Royal Icing Borders	2	Marzipan Flowers	2
Butter Cream Flowers	2	Royal Icing Flowers	2	Gum Trag Flowers	2
3-D Figure Piping	2	Royal Icing Filigrees	2	Pastillage Projects	2
Birthday Cakes	2	Special Order Cakes	2	Wedding Cakes	2
TOTAL	8	TOTAL	8	TOTAL	8
Borders		**Borders**		**Borders**	
Shell, Reverse & Rope	3	Fine Drop Scroll Piping	3	Shell with Double Trellis	3
Tripple Reverse Shell	3	Side Scroll Designs	3	Shell with Tripple Trellis	3
Eliptical Shell Border	3	Ring Border with Trellis	3	Star with Point Trellis	3
Basket Weave Construction	3	Vine Cluster Border	3	Inverted & Vertical Shells	3
TOTAL	12	TOTAL	12	TOTAL	12
Flowers		**Flowers**		**Flowers**	
Sweetpeas, ½ rose, rose buds	2	Lily of the Valley	2	Marzipan Roses	2
½ Carnation, Full Carnation	2	Wisteria (Side of Cake)	2	Trag Rose, Calyx, Stem	2
Small Roses, Large Roses	2	Poinsettia and Holly	2	Trag Sweetpea Cluster	2

Pansy, Mums, Daffodils	2	Daisy, Easter Lily	2	Trag Hawaiin Orchid	2
Pine Cone, Apple Blossoms	2	Six Part Orchid	2	Selection of Flowers	2
TOTAL	10	TOTAL	10	TOTAL	10

Fine Pastries | Fine Pastries | Fine Pastries

Carolines, Croquenbouche	6	Genoise - Plain & Filled	3	Short Pastry Pate Brisee	4
Swans & Baskets	4	Meringue Francaise	3	Swiss Meringue Suisse	4
Ice Cream, Sponge Roulades	6	Paris - Brest	4	Mousse au chocolat	4
Fancy Tea Sweet Pastries	24	Chantilly Creams	8	Miniature Fruit Tartlets	18
Sacher Torte I thru V	10	Assorted Fancy Cakes	32	Assorted Cheese Cakes	20
TOTAL	50	TOTAL	50	TOTAL	50

GRAND TOTAL   120   GRAND TOTAL   120   GRAND TOTAL   120

Baking Instructor Adolph (Steve) Volk
West Valley Jr. College (1965 thru 1966)
Saratoga Campus, California

3rd Semester, 20 Students
Name (100 subjects) we studied &
worked at in Classroom projects

Final exam from class feedback and student's notebooks. Five questions per student. The following information is not in order.

1. Orientation & Objectives: Demos, speakers, and hands on learning.
2. Safety & Sanitation: Book & classroom study. Info from the Health Dept.
3. Maintain Good Personal Hygiene at all times. Your hands carry many germs.
4. Safety Work Habits: If you don't know or understand this it will be reviewed in class.
5. How to Safely Use Baking Equipment: Prior to use safety will be explained step by step.
6. Demo of All Equipment. Pulling electric plugs before cleaning & how to clean.
7. Bake Shop Ingredients: Inventory before & after class. Ingredients needed for next class.
8. Food Storage Rotation & Cleaning as needed for prevention of spoilage
9. Food Cost Control: Items needed for class and extra projects.
10. Schedule of Training & Time: See chalkboard for assignments.
11. Weights & Measures for Mixing: Check to see if you have ingredients needed for project.
12. Reading & Understanding Recipes: Check your recipe. One mistake it one to many.
13. Dividing or Increasing Recipes: Math project and homework needed.
14. Recipe in Percentages; Flour Weight. Math project and homework needed.
15. Proper Mixing of Ingredients: Explain in writing on recipe you want to mix. Home work.
16. Bench Work, Speed & Quality: Clean up as you work.
17. Basic Ovens & Baking Procedures: Explain in writing, include safety. Home work.
18. Oven Safety, Temperatures & Timing: Relate to recipe you worked on. Home work.
19. Schedule of Yeast Breads: Advance class... include make-up of tail bread. Fun class.
20. Dinner Rolls (hard & soft), Kneading: Fancy rolls for hotels & country clubs.
21. Quick Breads, Muffins & Biscuits; for customers bread basket, caterers, ship lines.
22. Danish (make-up) Retarder, Proof Box: Bench for coffee shops & restaurants.
23. Safety & Demo of Sheeter: Cleaning before and after use, including storage.
24. Student Use of Sheeter: Two at a time with instruction and supervision.
25. Danish Bench Work, All Types: From scratch, including frozen dough imported.
26. Safety of Donut Fryer: Hot grease danger. In case of fire smother with lid. No water. Use salt.

27. Project Cleaning of Fryer: Replace 20% of fat, strain thru valve with strainer & cheese Cloth.
28. Student Use of Donut Fryer: Two at a time supervised.
29. Student Cleaning (on going): Bench, tools, floor, & storage area.
30. Sponge Cakes & Jelly Rolls (basic): Including press cakes, 8 layers pressed over night
31. White, Chocolate & Marble Cake: Using Wilton novelty pans. Info on copyrights.
32. Angle, Spice & Carrot Cake, Fruit Cake: Holidays etc.
33. Assorted Bake Shop Cookies, Decorating them & cooky baskets.
34. Fruit Bars, Nut Bars, Brownies & Fudge Bars. Learn to cut for 2 oz/3oz/4oz.
35. Ice Box Cut Out Cookies: Novelty cookies with special cutters and decorations.

All This Information Is From The Students Notebooks, > As They Wrote It.

36. Special Baked Goods to Learn: Signature pastries & your own recipes.
37. Swedish Tarts, Eclairs & Cream Puffs Croakenbush, decorated with boiled sugar etc.
38. Press Cake & Petit Fours: Use of apricot glaze, marzipan,, fondant plus décor.
39. Review all Safety Procedures: Safety, sanitation, hygiene... on going.
40. Butter Cream Icings, Rolled Fondant, Whipped Cream.
41. Use of Fondants, Glaze Icings, Ganasche, Royal Icing, Marzipan etc.
42. Merinque, Royal Icing, Stay Shine, Fen Cakes & Pastries.
43. Use of Food Colors: Paste, Liquid, Spray and Powder, oil or water.
44. Review & Information covering Baking & Projects, including Gingerbread Houses
45. Scratch vs. Mixes: Frozen items, saving time & labor.
46. Frozen Baked Goods & Refrigeration of Goods: Proper temperatures & storage time.
47. Frozen Eggs, Whites, Yolks vs. Fresh Eggs also How to Handle Powdered Eggs.
48. Prepare Pans for Baking, Grease, Flour, Dust, Pie tins, use cake crumbs on bottom of tin.
49. Pan Extenders, also Parchment Liners.
50. Review Ovens & Convection Ovens. Lower temp. for convection ovens.
51. Regulate Oven Temp. Draft & Thermostat Controls as needed.
52. Bread Ovens Have Steam Piped In Safely: Read oven manual before using.
53. Schedule of Training for Cake Decorating: For quality & timing your speed.
54. Demo of Cake Decorating Equip: You can do this on a 10" cake dummy.
55. Use of Kopy Kake Machine & Air Brush: Use sheet of paper to learn air brushing.
56. Silk Screen, Spray Colors & Piping Gel Lines for transfers onto cake icing.
57. Piping Gel Transfers, Rice Paper Art & Cocoa Painting on a 10" cake dummy.
58. Different Paper Cones & Uses of Pastry Bags, cleaning & storage while working.
59. Types of Color, Blending of Color: example yellow & blue make green, red & yellow make orange.

60. Powder, Paste, Liquid Paste, Liquid Spray can be mixed in paper cups.
61. Gingerbread Houses in fall class/Panoramic Easters Eggs in spring class.
62. Review Set-up Pastry Bags & Tubes & sanitation.
63. Review Folding Paper Cones & Use for storage for next shift or day. Cover with towel.
64. Use of Turn Table & Different Tools you are unfamiliar with.
65. Special Pans & Cut Out Patterns for Gingerbread Houses and cake decorating.
66. Cake Decorating Tubes with Control & Quality... right size & right pressure.
67. Review Shell, Rope, & Reverse Borders... right & left handed. Surprising results.
68. Triple Reverse & Royal Icing Shell Borders... Practice on cake boards & rounds.
69. 3-D Figures & Buttercream Figures... lots of fun.
70. Piping Clowns, Elephants & Balloons... for party cakes.
71. Royal Icing (flood work) Transfers: Piping gel squares, using 5 colors.
72. Review Kopy Kake, Silk Screens, Air Gun and how to clean.
73. Icing on Cardboards & Styrofoam for practice, practice & practice.
74. Combing in Background with Colors then add on your own art work.
75. Special Flower Icing & Tubes... more pressure if needed. Do not overfill piping bags.
76. Three Types of Icing Sweet Peas, Pine Cones and other flowers to demo.
77. Rose Buds (closed & opened) 2/3 Petals (1-3-5) method, using nail or stick.
78. Half Roses, Half Carnations & Tea Roses, blending colors in pastry bag.
79. American Beauty Roses, Cabbage Roses, white, yellow, white, pink, white, (repeat)

With Written Hand Outs, In Our Last Class, We Review What We Had Learn.

80. Assorted Mums, Daffodils, Pansies... just getting started.
81. Daisies, Poinsettias, Lily of the Valley etc.
82. Setting up, Icing & Filling Wedding Cakes crumb coating or using hot apricot to start.
83. Proper Balance, Dowels, Plates & Pins to stabilize for delivery.
84. Types of Wedding Cakes & Fountains.. advise not to use colors in fountains.
85. Side Borders, Vine Clusters & Cannelli.
86. Australian Rolled Fondant & African Wings needs much practice & patience.
87. Delivery of Wedding Cakes... repair kits, extra icing and icing flowers.
88. Review Filling & Splitting Cakes... wells for fillings, balance with pins & plates.
89. Understanding Counter Sales... a cooky for a child & samples on the counter.
90. Be Courteous and Understanding to Customers... they pay your wages.
91. Proper Telephone Skills, Write-up Orders... names & phone nos. always.
92. Cash Registers, Making Proper Change, coins first, bills next. Check the large ones.
93. Make up Displays, Labels, and Signs... comedy or colors attract.
94. Advance Classes in French Pastries.

95. Advance Project Classes & Skills.
96. Introduction to German, Swiss, English & Spanish Pastries.
97. Safety with Pulled Sugar & Ice Carvings... demo first, hands on next.
98. Culinary Art Shows & Entering same,,,
99. Joining Cake Decorating Clubs & Culinary Federation... ACF, RBA, ICES
100. Introduction to other programs, short classes, advanced classes by skilled food service Instructors. Info on other food service colleges, skill centers, private schools not to mention hotel training, basic and advanced.

The above information was copied and handed back to the student prior to the end of the semester. A copy was also given to the Dean of Education.

At West Valley College classes were from 7 to 10 PM, Monday thru Thursday for a period of 13 years (1965-1978). I then moved to Sacramento CA.

At Canada College I had two classes beginning at 8 am until 2 pm, Monday thru Tuesday for 6 years (1970-1976). Fund exhausted.

At Bakers Handcraft Training classes were 40 hours per week for a six month period. This school later became Pacific Coast College which lasted for 6 years.

The above are ideas for a new instructor or culinary class as a syllibis to introduce new programs.

Sincerely,

Adolph (Steve) Volk
ACF/CEPC/CCE/AAC/RBA Master Baker

Printed in the United States
By Bookmasters